TExES Technology Education 6-12 (171) Test

"You never fail until you stop trying" - Albert Einstein

For inquiries;
info@xmprep.com

TExES Technology Education 6-12 (171) Test #1

Test Taking Tips

☐ Take a deep breath and relax

☐ Read directions carefully

☐ Read the questions thoroughly

☐ Make sure you understand what is being asked

☐ Go over all of the choices before you answer

☐ Paraphrase the question

☐ Eliminate the options you know are wrong

☐ Check your work

☐ Think positively and do your best

Table of Contents

TEST DIRECTION

DIRECTIONS

Read the questions carefully and then choose the ONE best answer to each question.

Be sure to allocate your time carefully so you are able to complete the entire test within the testing session. You may go back and review your answers at any time.

You may use any available space in your test booklet for scratch work.

Questions in this booklet are not actual test questions but they are the samples for commonly asked questions.

This test aims to cover all topics which may appear on the actual test. However some topics may not be covered.

Studying this booklet will be preparing you for the actual test. It will not guarantee improving your test score but it will help you pass your exam on the first attempt.

Some useful tips for answering multiple choice questions;

- Start with the questions that you can easily answer.

- Underline the keywords in the question.

- Be sure to read all the choices given.

- Watch for keywords such as NOT, always, only, all, never, completely.

- Do not forget to answer every question.

1

Which of the following violates the copyright law when someone buys an image-editing software?

A) Copying the software onto a disk for a friend
B) Selling the software and the software's disk to a third party
C) Copying the software's disk to make a backup
D) Creating artwork with the application and selling it

2

"Technology in the classroom" generally means _____.

A) any type of technology, such as calculators, educational applets, etc., that serve as supplementary materials for learning
B) gadgets and devices that students bring to school
C) electric sharpeners and erasable ink
D) any type of technology that replaces the instructional role of teachers

3

Which of the following is chiefly responsible for the forward movement of a fixed-wing aircraft?

A) Thrust
B) Lift
C) Weight
D) Drag

4

The purpose of instructional objectives is:

A) To have the same ideas as the district's goals when it comes to student learning.
B) To have the school board develop you.
C) To be able to be applied to students with various levels of ability.
D) To reflect each teacher's personal way of teaching.

5

Which of the following plots results data for preproduction processes in advanced manufacturing?

A) Run-sequence plot x
B) Range chart
C) Pareto chart
D) X-bar chart

CONTINUE ▶

6

By adopting the Common Core Standards, a school most directly reflects the state's commitment to:

A) ensuring accountability for teachers, schools, and districts
B) guaranteeing that graduates have the knowledge and skills needed for college or career success
C) delivering culturally responsive instructions and address the students' diverse needs
D) strengthening collaboration with other states to improve learning achievement

7

Which of the following is an example of the power system found in an early 19th century railway steam locomotive engines?

A) Reaction engine
B) Internal combustion (IC) engine
C) External combustion (EC) engine
D) Rotary engine

8

Which of the following areas of study are the key concepts of guidance, control, suspension, propulsion, and support taught in?

A) Biotechnical systems
B) Integrated systems
C) Transportation
D) Manufacturing

9

Which of the following would be the main concern of community planners prior to the building of a car-manufacturing factory's plans for a new plant?

A) The operating hours of the plant
B) The employee's work environment at the plant
C) The quantity of materials to be kept in the plant
D) The plant's impact on the environment

CONTINUE ▶

10

In a large-scale commercial construction venture, which of the following is normally the first step that needs to be taken?

A) Applying for building permits and variances
B) Holding a discussion with the developer, designer, and contractor regarding the scope of the construction
C) Ordering the necessary materials for building the foundation
D) Drafting a contract specifying details of the building plan

11

Understanding and knowledge regarding which of the following is crucial in the successful design of graphic communications messages?

A) The limitations of the printer
B) The capabilities of the designer
C) Current technologies
D) The nature of the audience

12

What assessment measures a student's ability to learn in a certain situation?

A) CBM (Curriculum-Based Measure).
B) Diagnostic assessment.
C) Dynamic assessment.
D) An aptitude test.

13

He introduced the World Wide Web (www) way back in 1991.

A) Steve Jobs
B) Dwight D. Eisenhower
C) Bill Gates
D) Tim Berners-Lee

14

The image above depicts a type of mechanical stress.

Which of the following does the image denote?

A) Torsion
B) Compression
C) Shear
D) Tension

15

A teacher has implemented learning objectives for a unit of study. Which of the following steps should the teacher take next?

A) Put in order the activities to help students meet the learning objectives.
B) Implement strategies for presenting concepts related to the learning objectives.
C) Identify skills that students will need to develop in meeting the learning objectives.
D) Determine how to evaluate students' mastery of the learning objectives.

16

Signature-based detection methods refer to the methods for the detection of attacks by looking for specific patterns, such as byte sequences in network traffic, or known malicious instruction sequences used by malware.

However, its greatest drawback is that the software will _____.

A) Block incoming data from the network server
B) Fail to identify new or unknown viruses
C) Require frequent scans of all executable files
D) Delete essential files that are not infected

17

SSL is the standard security technology for establishing an encrypted link between a web server and a browser. This link ensures that all data passed between the web server and browsers remain private and integral.

What does SSL stand for?

A) Secure system login
B) System socket layer
C) Secure socket layer
D) Secure system login

18

A manufacturing system is a method of organizing production. Many types of manufacturing systems are in place, including assembly lines, batch production and computer-integrated manufacturing, or even mass production manufacturing and custom manufacturing. Which of the options below is an advantage of using mass production over custom?

A) Feedback can be provided to the workers by customers.
B) Faster production and lower cost.
C) Workers can learn important skills.
D) Certain products can be more easily modified at the request of customers.

19

An address book or a name and address book (NAB) is a book or a database used for storing entries called contacts.

The purpose of an address book in an email package is _____.

A) To keep a list of previously visited URL's
B) To keep a list of all contacts and their email addresses
C) To attach a file like a word document to a message
D) To attach an email signature to an email

20

Communication Cycle refers to the transfer of information from one person to the another through a proper cycle.

Which of the following is essential component of communication cycle?

A) A message
B) An email account
C) An internet connection
D) An interpreter

21

Which of the following is not correct about communication?

A) Nonverbal communication is the use of body movements to send a message.
B) If a speaker uses graphs, charts he is using an assertion of logic.
C) It is never appropriate to use obscene language in a speech.
D) Pitch has a psychological effect that influences how people perceive your speech's content.

22

By considering which of the following first can the teacher prepare an effective lesson oan for a new instructional unit?

A) Unit activities best for individual and group work
B) The ways unit supports the goals of the district curriculum in this subject area.
C) Background knowledge the students already have with regard to the unit topic.
D) The most efficient way to evaluate students' achievement of unit objectives.

23

Several instructors are developing software with the goal of improving students' drafting skills.

Which of the following is the first appropriate step that the instructors should take?

A) Determine the learning objectives intended for the software
B) Download the most widely used software for evaluation
C) Decide the most appropriate user interface (UI) for the software
D) Determine the importance of drafting skills through a survey

24

Computer virus is a piece of code that is capable of copying itself and typically has a detrimental effect, such as corrupting the system or destroying data. In 1983, _____ was the first to offer a definition of the term 'computer virus'.

A) Norton
B) Cohen
C) Mcafee
D) Smith

25

An instruction is an order given to a computer processor by a computer program.

Which of the following would allow users to interactively send instructions (such as printing and closing a window) to a computer using graphical icons?

A) GUI
B) Keyboard
C) Commands
D) Printer

26

A reference guide has just been updated. Upon accessing the file, a few employees are confused about which of the printed documents is the latest update.

What feature should be included in the reference guide to avoid this confusion?

A) The names of the authors
B) Version number
C) The copyright information
D) Data printed

28

A CD player is an electronic device that plays audio compact discs, which are a digital optical disc data storage format. For reproducing sound, the CD audio player uses a _____.

A) Titanium Needle
B) Barium Titanium Ceramic
C) Laser Beam
D) Quartz Cristal

27

Which of the following terms is not defined correctly?

A) Development is the continuous process of change that all humans experience during their life.
B) Learning is the change of behaviors, thoughts or emotions based on genetics.
C) Growth is the physical process of development.
D) Maturation is the physical, emotional or intellectual process of development.

29

Volatile memory is computer storage that only maintains its data while the device is powered.

In which of the following can we classify volatile memory?

A) Read-Only Memory (ROM)
B) Random-Access Memory (RAM)
C) Hard Drive
D) Cache

30

In contrast to finite energy sources like fossil fuels, renewable energy sources naturally regenerate over time.

Which of the following is an example of a renewable energy source?

A) Oil
B) Coal
C) Natural gas
D) Wood

31

MAC is a term used defined as _____.

A) Memory address corruption
B) A computer made by Apple
C) Mediocre Apple Computer
D) Media Access Control

32

Which type of performance assessment lets the teacher decide what the students are able to do for long periods of time?

A) Extended performance assessment
B) Individual performance assessment
C) Restricted-response performance assessment
D) Authentic performance assessment

33

The teacher always begins regular class meetings by giving individual students an opportunity to thank a classmate for assistance with a difficult or challenging task.

Which of the following outcomes does it have to begin a class meeting in this way?

A) A positive learning environment that fosters excellence
B) Students' self-monitoring of their own behavior
C) A supportive and caring classroom community
D) High expectations for their learning

Solid-state storage is a type of non-volatile computer storage that stores and retrieves digital information using only electronic circuits, without any involvement of moving mechanical parts.

Which of the following is a characteristic of Solid State Storage devices?

A) They have no moving parts
B) Data cannot be erased from them once written.
C) They have greater storage capacity than Hard disks.
D) They consume a lot of power.

Computer software is said to have Internal Documentation if the notes on how and why various parts of code operate is included within the source code as comments.

Which of the following is the primary reason for producing internal program documentation?

A) Tracing the execution by printing output at critical branching points
B) Increasing program reliability by reporting and storing error codes
C) Providing explanations of code segments for maintenance and updates
D) Reducing execution time by improving memory allocation and usage

Educational Psychology is the study of how humans learn and retain knowledge, primarily in educational settings like classrooms. It includes social, emotional and cognitive learning processes.

Which of the following about Educational Esychology is not correct?

A) The responsibility of learning falls on the learner rather than the teacher according to the Constructivist perspective

B) Albert Bandura contributed a lot to the Social-Cognitive Educational Psychology.

C) Learning occurs through stage-like processes according to the Developmental Educational Psychology.

D) Learning occurs through observation according to the Cognitive Educational Psychology.

SECTION 1

#	Answer	Topic	Subtopic		#	Answer	Topic	Subtopic		#	Answer	Topic	Subtopic		#	Answer	Topic	Subtopic
1	A	TB	SB1		10	B	TB	SB2		19	B	TB	SB1		28	C	TB	SB1
2	A	TA	SA2		11	S	TB	SB2		20	A	TA	SA1		29	B	TB	SB1
3	A	TB	SB2		12	C	TA	SA2		21	D	TA	SA1		30	D	TB	SB3
4	A	TA	SA2		13	D	TA	SA1		22	C	TA	SA2		31	D	TB	SB1
5	A	TB	SB2		14	A	TB	SB2		23	A	TA	SA2		32	A	TA	SA2
6	B	TA	SA2		15	C	TA	SA2		24	B	TA	SA1		33	C	TA	SA2
7	C	TB	SB3		16	B	TB	SB1		25	A	TB	SB1		34	A	TB	SB1
8	C	TB	SB2		17	C	TB	SB1		26	B	TB	SB1		35	C	TB	SB1
9	D	TB	SB2		18	B	TA	SA1		27	B	TA	SA2		36	D	TA	SA2

Topics & Subtopics

Code	Description		Code	Description
SA1	Technology & Society		SB3	Energy Power & Transportation
SA2	Pedagogical & Professional Studies		TA	Education
SB1	Information & Communication Technologies		TB	Technology
SB2	Manufacturing & Construction			

CONTINUE ▶

TEST DIRECTION

DIRECTIONS

Read the questions carefully and then choose the ONE best answer to each question.

Be sure to allocate your time carefully so you are able to complete the entire test within the testing session. You may go back and review your answers at any time.

You may use any available space in your test booklet for scratch work.

Questions in this booklet are not actual test questions but they are the samples for commonly asked questions.

This test aims to cover all topics which may appear on the actual test. However some topics may not be covered.

Studying this booklet will be preparing you for the actual test. It will not guarantee improving your test score but it will help you pass your exam on the first attempt.

Some useful tips for answering multiple choice questions;

- Start with the questions that you can easily answer.

- Underline the keywords in the question.

- Be sure to read all the choices given.

- Watch for keywords such as NOT, always, only, all, never, completely.

- Do not forget to answer every question.

CONTINUE ▶

1

The United States Department of Transportation (USDOT) hazmat placard above symbolizes which of the following?

A) Corrosive substance
B) Electrical hazard
C) Recycling
D) Biohazard

2

Which of the following is the structure that provides vertical support in the construction of a house?

A) Headers
B) Studs
C) Joists
D) Rafters

3

What does the acronym "OS" stand for?

A) Open software
B) Operating system
C) Optical Sensor
D) Order of significance

4

Why is using a network switch more preferrable than using a newtwork hub?

A) Because a networ switch reduces the network traffic
B) Because a network switch connects a computer directly to the internet
C) Because a network switch prevents all viruses from spreading
D) Because a network switch strengthens password security

5

A computer storage device is any type of hardware that stores data. Which of the following storage devices allows access to information in a sequential mode?

A) Hard disk
B) DVD
C) CD-R
D) Magnetic tape

6

Which factor has been most responsible for decisions to place greater emphasis on developing students' problem-solving and decision-making skills across the curriculum?

A) the increasing influence of media in teaching and learning
B) The change in occupational demands in both local and global societies
C) The increase in educational accountability of every school
D) The change in inclusion practices in every school

7

Understanding and knowledge regarding which of the following is crucial in the successful design of graphic communications messages?

A) The limitations of the printer
B) The capabilities of the designer
C) Current technologies
D) The nature of the audience

8

How can you successfully convert an image from BMP to JPEG format?

A) By changing the image file extension
B) By compressing the file
C) By using the "Save As" command
D) By renaming the image

CONTINUE ▶

9

A rural school seeks to increase its access to technological resources for teaching and learning. However, the school is significantly experiencing funding problems.

Which action should the school administrators do to achieve this goal?

A) Collaborate with educators from the more affluent and technologically advanced schools to learn various strategies.
B) Seek support from local businesses that may have interest in having partnerships in achieving the school's goal.
C) Cut other areas of the school's budget plan and use it to increase the technology funding.
D) Solicit for public assistance in raising funds for the school through publicizing its needs in newspapers and other local media.

10

Which type of engineer among the following is most likely involved in the planning of a large dam's construction?

A) Systems engineer
B) Architectural engineer
C) Mechanical engineer
D) Civil engineer

11

Kilobyte is a multiple of the unit byte for digital information. How many bits are there in a KiloByte? —1000

A) 1000
B) 8192
C) 1024
D) 8024

Your colleague happily shared his view of technology, saying "Technology is great! Using technology in every lesson keeps the kids so occupied I barely have to teach!"

Why should you not totally agree with his comment?

A) Because technology should be used as an enhancement and supplement to effective teaching and learning, without replacing the instructional role of teachers.
B) Because technology should never be used for instruction but only as a recreational tool.
C) Because technology should always be used as often as possible and he is proof that it works.
D) Because technology distracts students and hinders learning.

Curriculum can be defined as the totality of student experiences that occur in the educational process.

Which of the following about curriculum is not correct?

A) Curriculum planning is important because it makes classroom discipline easier.
B) A curriculum map is an ever evolving document that should be generally followed based on the needs of the students.
C) Big ideas are important in curriculum planning because it helps teacher figure out what's most important about a curriculum.
D) Modern curriculum models are often a blend of process and product.

14

Asperger Syndrome (AS) is a neurobiological disorder on the higher-functioning end of the autism spectrum.

Which of the following is characteristic of a child with Asperger's Syndrome?

A) Difficulty with social interactions such as speaking and forming complete sentences.
B) High academic performance and cognitive development.
C) Inability to acquire new information in classes such as mathematics.
D) Delayed mental development and motor skills development.

15

An effective teacher engages all students and provides a learning environment where all students can learn.

Which of the following is a strategy used in effective teaching?

A) Breaking complex material down and making difficult topics easy to understand
B) Getting feedback from students and motivating them.
C) Promoting student interest and giving plenty of examples to clarify the topic.
D) All of the above

16

The internet or Internet is the global system of interconnected computer networks that use the Internet protocol suite (TCP/IP) to link devices worldwide. Its original purpose was which of the following?

A) Global marketing and business transactions.
B) Allow people from all over the globe to easily share their thoughts and ideas.
C) Distribution of academic research papers.
D) Sustain the connectivity of US defense computers.

17

Computer data is information processed or stored by a computer such as text, documents, images, audio clips, software programs, or other types of data.

How is computer data represented inside the computer?

A) Byte system
B) Binary system
C) Hexadecimal system
D) Logical System

18

Which of the following is not true?

A) The most significant quality of a good assessment is validity.

B) An assessment is the process of gathering and discussing information from multiple and diverse sources in order to develop a deep understanding of what students know, understand, and can do with their knowledge as a result of their educational experiences.

C) A standardized test is any form of test that requires all test takers to answer the same questions, or a selection of questions from common bank of questions.

D) While interpreting raw scores, knowledge of basic statistics is essential.

19

In terms of social development of nine year-old students, which of the following teacher strategies is likely to have the most positive influence?

A) Emphasizing student-led activities

B) Encouraging students during challenging activities

C) Giving chance for students to express their feelings freely in the classroom.

D) Assigning cooperative rather than competitive student activities

20

There are six major categories of computers which are based on differences in size, speed, processing capabilities, and price.

In which category of computers do desktop computers, notebooks (laptops) and Personal Digital Assistants (PDA's) fall?

A) Micro computers

B) Supercomputers

C) Mainframe computers

D) Mini computers

21

A file format is the structure of how information is stored in a computer file.

Which file format would be the most appropriate when data from a spreadsheet needs to be imported into a database package?

A) CSV

B) RTF

C) HTML

D) PDF

22

In a manufacturing laboratory, a student asks his teacher what assembly procedures should be used when solving a fabrication problem.

Which of the following would be the teacher's best response?

A) Provide possible assembly procedures for the student to select
B) Ask the student to make their own judgment and decide
C) Provide an opinion on the best assembly procedure for the problem
D) Use leading questions to guide the student in analyzing the merits of different assembly procedures

23

PPTP is an obsolete method for implementing virtual private networks, with many known security issues.

What does PPTP stand for?

A) Point to Point Transfer Protocol
B) Point to Point Traffic Protocol
C) Point to Point Tunneling Protocol
D) Point to Point Transmission Protocol

24

A student would want to use technology as a learning tool throughout the school year.

Which is the BEST example of how this student can accomplish this goal?

A) Make a poster to illustrate the student's ideas about an article.
B) The student uses a smartphone to call a tutor to help her answer a quiz.
C) The student makes a report and a presentation in her computer.
D) The student uses the refernces found in her textbook to find additional resources for a project.

25

The engineering design process is also known as a series of steps that engineers follow to come up with a solution to a problem. Many times this solution involves designing a product (like a machine or computer code) that meets certain criteria arid/or accomplishes a certain task. Out of the options below, what is the last step in this process?

A) Creating solution
B) Testing and analysis
C) Generating idea
D) Improving the design

CONTINUE ▶

An internal modem is a network device that is contained on an expansion board that plugs into the motherboard.

An internal modem is usually connected to a computer via a(an) _____.

A) PCI Express slot
B) PCI slot
C) AGP slot
D) USB port

A motherboard is one of the most essential parts of a computer system. It holds together many of the crucial components of a computer, including the central processing unit (CPU), memory and connectors for input and output devices.

Which of the following would indicate that the motherboard battery has failed?

A) Files on the hard disk are lost and corrupted.
B) Hardware settings, including virtual memory reverts to default values.
C) Operating system passwords are lost.
D) Hardware settings, including the current date and time reverts to default values.

Curriculum design is a statement which identifies the elements of the curriculum, shows what their relationships are to each other. It also indicates the principles and the requirements of organization for the administrative conditions under which it is to operate. Which of the following about curriculum design is not correct?

A) Curriculum is the stuff teachers teach.
B) Curriculum models provide a framework for curriculum guides.
C) Backward design in curriculum planning is designing the end of the day before designing the beginning of the day
D) Curriculum planning helps make sure teaching on a daily basis has a larger purpose.

Technology is the collection of techniques, skills, methods and processes used in the production of goods or services or in the accomplishment of objectives, such as scientific investigation. Technology can be the knowledge of techniques, processes, and the like, or it can be embedded in machines which can be operated without detailed knowledge of their workings. Examples of these are: paper, matches, seismological detectors, wheelbarrow, sliding calipers. Which ancient civilization developed all of these?

A) Egyptians
B) Endulus
C) Maya
D) Chinese

A punch card is a piece of stiff paper that can be used to contain digital information represented by the presence or absence of holes in predefined positions.

Who is credited with the idea of using punch cards to control patterns in a waving machine?

A) Hollerith
B) Babbage
C) Pascal
D) Jacquard

Computer software is a set of instructions and associated documentation that tells a computer what to do or how to perform a task.

An English language learner is searching for a computer software to help him make connections between written and spoken English. Which of the following types of computer software would be most effective?

A) automated translation
B) word prediction
C) speech synthesizer
D) sound recording

BIOS is the program a personal computer's microprocessor uses to get the computer system started after you turn it on.

The BIOS stands for Basic Input Output System. It is found in the_____ of the computer and is the first piece of software that is run by the computer.

A) ROM
B) CMOS
C) MBR
D) RAM

SECTION 2

#	Answer	Topic	Subtopic		#	Answer	Topic	Subtopic		#	Answer	Topic	Subtopic		#	Answer	Topic	Subtopic
1	A	TA	SA1		9	B	TA	SA1		17	B	TB	SB1		25	D	TB	SB2
2	B	TB	SB2		10	D	TB	SB2		18	D	TA	SA2		26	B	TB	SB1
3	B	TB	SB1		11	B	TB	SB1		19	D	TA	SA2		27	D	TB	SB1
4	A	TB	SB1		12	A	TA	SA2		20	A	TB	SB1		28	C	TA	SA2
5	D	TB	SB1		13	A	TA	SA2		21	A	TB	SB1		29	A	TA	SA1
6	B	TA	SA1		14	A	TA	SA2		22	D	TB	SB2		30	D	TA	SA1
7	D	TB	SB1		15	D	TA	SA2		23	C	TB	SB1		31	C	TA	SA2
8	C	TB	SB1		16	D	TA	SA1		24	C	TA	SA2		32	A	TB	SB1

Topics & Subtopics

Code	Description		Code	Description
SA1	Technology & Society		SB2	Manufacturing & Construction
SA2	Pedagogical & Professional Studies		TA	Education
SB1	Information & Communication Technologies		TB	Technology

CONTINUE ▶

TEST DIRECTION

DIRECTIONS

Read the questions carefully and then choose the ONE best answer to each question.

Be sure to allocate your time carefully so you are able to complete the entire test within the testing session. You may go back and review your answers at any time.

You may use any available space in your test booklet for scratch work.

Questions in this booklet are not actual test questions but they are the samples for commonly asked questions.

This test aims to cover all topics which may appear on the actual test. However some topics may not be covered.

Studying this booklet will be preparing you for the actual test. It will not guarantee improving your test score but it will help you pass your exam on the first attempt.

Some useful tips for answering multiple choice questions;

- Start with the questions that you can easily answer.

- Underline the keywords in the question.

- Be sure to read all the choices given.

- Watch for keywords such as NOT, always, only, all, never, completely.

- Do not forget to answer every question.

CONTINUE ▶

1

Which of the following plots results data for preproduction processes in advanced manufacturing?

A) Run-sequence plot x
B) Range chart
C) Pareto chart
D) X-bar chart

2

Mark intends to build a garage and is determining the materials he needs for the garage's floor. It is important that the material Mark chooses should be resistant to which of the following?

A) Shear
B) Torsion
C) Tension
D) Compression

3

In designing a doghouse, which of the following would be the first step in the design process?

A) Purchasing the required materials for building
B) Determine the measurement of the dog and the materials for the interior
C) Acquiring the necessary tools for building
D) Identifying the aesthetic concerns of the exterior

4

A measurement that shows the "average differences" from what most people score on a test is called _____.

A) standard deviation
B) mean
C) median
D) mode

5

Which type of engineer among the following is most likely involved in the planning of a large dam's construction?

A) Systems engineer
B) Architectural engineer
C) Mechanical engineer
D) Civil engineer

CONTINUE ▶

6

In what way are science and technolgy related?

A) Science and technology are not related, each deal with separate things.
B) Technology is the application of scientific knowledge for practical purposes in the society.
C) Science is the application of technology for practical purposes in the society.
D) None of the above.

7

According to Perkins intelligence has three dimensions? Which of the following gives these components?

A) Reflective, Neural and Experiential
B) Neural, Experiential and Emotional
C) Neural, Emotional and Experiential
D) Emotional, Experiential and Reflective

8

Which approach out of the following has been known to give the most effective results when it comes to increasing group productivity?

A) Select a bigger team, since the pool of ideas would therefore be bigger.
B) Swap roles between members, therefore a supervisor wouldn't be the one to always make the last decision.
C) Select a diverse team in terms of gender, ethnicity, age, and work experience.
D) Select members that together form an equilibrium of the criteria of the HBDI (Herrmann Brain Dominance Instrument) system.

9

The voltage between two points in a circuit is 5,000 volts.

Which could be the parameters of the simple circuit?

A) The simple circuit should have a current of 20 amperes and a resistance of 250 ohms.
B) The simple circuit should have a current of 20 amperes and a resistance of 100,000 ohms.
C) The simple circuit should have a current of 20 ohms and a resistance of 250 amperes.
D) The simple circuit should have a current of 100,000 amperes and a resistance of 20 ohms.

10

An output device is any device used to send data from a computer to another device or user. Which of the following is not an output device?

A) Plotter
B) Printer
C) Monitor
D) Touchscreen

11

Which type of wall provides the support needed to withstand weight from a building's ceiling and roof?

A) Stud-support
B) Rafter-plate
C) Load-bearing
D) Ceiling-joist

12

What is the primary function of a transformer?

A) To increase, decrease or maintain the voltage amount
B) To increase the amount of current passing through the wire
C) To block the electricity flow
D) To ground an electrical circuit in case of a current surge

13

A raw score represents _____.

A) a family of scores that allow us to make comparisons between test scores.
B) the average performance at age and grade levels.
C) how close to the average, or mean, the student's score fall.
D) the number of items a student answers correctly without adjustment for guessing.

14

Schema is an abstract concept in cognitive development, which was first used by Piaget. He emphasized the importance of schemas, and described how they were developed or acquired.

Which of the following defines schema best?

A) It is a cognitive framework or concept that helps organize and interpret information.
B) It defines the process of saving knowledge in the brain.
C) It refers to the first phase in cognitive development.
D) It is a term used to explain how the brain develops.

15

In computer hardware and software development, testing is used at key checkpoints in the overall process to determine whether objectives are being met.

Which of the following is NOT a type of testing?

A) Testing sample data on the computer
B) Manual Testing with sample data
C) Sample Checking
D) Testing by a group of users

16

Which of the following defines the role of a teacher in a student-centered environment?

A) Law enforcer who makes sure students are following the rules and regulations.
B) Co-teacher who works alongside the students to deliver lessons.
C) Organizer who monitors and supports student activities.
D) Dictator who tells students what to do and controls all their actions.

17

Computer company is a commercial entity involved in the computer industry. Which American computer company is called Big Blue?

A) IBM
B) Tandy Svenson
C) Compaq Corp
D) Microsoft

18

Networking software is a foundational element for any network. It helps administrators deploy, manage and monitor a network.

Which country created the most used networking software in 1980's?

A) Microsoft
B) Sun
C) Novell
D) IBM

19

An error is a term used to describe any issue that arises unexpectedly that cause a computer to not function properly.

The omission of a semicolon at the end of a statement in C++ is an example of a _____ error.

A) syntax
B) calculation
C) loop
D) direct

20

Electronic mail (email) is a method of exchanging messages between people using electronics.

Which of the following statements is true about email history?

A) The first email was sent by David Crocker in 1963.
B) The first email was sent by Gregor Maxwell in 1969.
C) The first email was sent by Ray Tomlinson in 1971.
D) The first email was sent by Gray Tomlinson in 1974.

21

Which of the following organizations could help a high school teacher to pursue professional development opportunities for integrating computational thinking and programming concepts into his class?

A) Computer Science Teachers Association
B) Special Interest Group on Computer Science Education
C) Association for the Advancement of Computing in Education
D) International Society for Technology in Education

22

A computer communication defines rules and conventions for communication between network devices. Communication between computers is achieved by networking computers together using connecting devices and setting up of strict rules for communication to take place.

These 'rules' are more appropriately termed as _____.

A) Internet
B) Protocols
C) Browser
D) Web

23

Which of the following about development is not correct?

A) B.F. Skinner has contributed to the behaviorist perspective of Educational Psychology.
B) Learning how to do addition is an example of cognitive development.
C) Environment influences a person's genes. This belief is an example of the interaction of DNA and heredity.
D) Emotional development is about understanding emotions while social development is about learning to interact with others.

24

The Open Systems Interconnection model is a conceptual model that characterizes and standardizes the communication functions of a telecommunication or computing system without regard to their underlying internal structure and technology.

Which of the following layers of the Open Systems Interconnection model is wireless network technology implemented?

A) Session
B) Data link
C) Application
D) Physical

25

Which of the following would be the main concern of community planners prior to the building of a car-manufacturing factory's plans for a new plant?

A) The operating hours of the plant
B) The employee's work environment at the plant
C) The quantity of materials to be kept in the plant
D) The plant's impact on the environment

26

Creativity development is a nonlinear and multifaceted process starting early in life.

Which of the following about creativity development and intelligence of a child is not correct?

A) Sternberg proposed The Triarchic Theory
B) Child's creativity can be assessed by The Torrance Test
C) Adoption studies show evidence of a genetic influence on intelligence
D) Crystallized intelligence refers to the knowledge that remains stable over the years.

27

What should teachers keep in mind when designing instruction?

A) Not all kids are on the same level.
B) Instructional planning isn't as crucial as it is believed.
C) All students understand the same way.
D) The previous experiences of students aren't the base of learning.

28

An email address identifies an email box to which email messages are delivered. An email address is made up of a local-part, an @ symbol, then a case-insensitive domain.

In what year was the @ chosen for its use in email address?

A) 1972
B) 1984
C) 1980
D) 1976

29

A printer is an external hardware output device that takes the electronic data stored on a computer or other device and generates a hard copy of it.

Which of the following printers are known to press characters or dots against an inked ribbon onto a paper by means of a mechanical head of retracting pins?

A) Ink-Jet
B) Dot-matrix
C) Thermal
D) Laser

The mouse, sometimes called a pointer, is a hand-operated input device used to manipulate objects on a computer screen.

Which of the following types of mouse is a battery-powered device that transmits data using wireless technology such as radio waves or infrared light waves?

A) Cordless Mouse
B) Trackball
C) Optical Mouse
D) Mechanical Mouse

Vygotsky is an educational psychologist who is well known with his sociocultural theory. According to this theory social interaction leads to continuous step-by-step changes in children's thought and behavior that can vary greatly from culture to culture.

Which of the following about cognitive development and Vygotsky's theory is not correct?

A) Vygotsky used a sociocultural perspective in his theory of cognitive development.
B) Staying cognitively active is helpful for maintaining both fluid and crystallized intelligence.
C) According to Vygotsky, scaffolding is the process of constructing an internal representation of external physical objects or actions.
D) Lev Vygotsky is most well-known for a cultural-historical theory of cognitive development emphasizing social interactions and culture.

A rubric is typically an evaluation tool or set of guidelines used to promote the consistent application of learning expectations, learning objectives, or learning standards in the classroom, or to measure their attainment against a consistent set of criteria.

A teacher would like to develop a rubric for assessing students' computer programs that students will be able to explain how their programs work. Which of the following rubric components could be most effective?

A) The code variables are declared using the correct data types.
B) The program outputs the correct solution to the problem.
C) The program compiles without any syntax or runtime errors.
D) The code contains clear and appropriate internal documentation.

SECTION 3

#	Answer	Topic	Subtopic	#	Answer	Topic	Subtopic	#	Answer	Topic	Subtopic	#	Answer	Topic	Subtopic
1	A	TB	SB2	9	A	TB	SB3	17	A	TA	SA1	25	D	TB	SB2
2	D	TB	SB2	10	D	TB	SB1	18	C	TA	SA1	26	D	TA	SA2
3	B	TB	SB2	11	C	TB	SB2	19	A	TB	SB1	27	A	TA	SA2
4	A	TA	SA2	12	A	TB	SB3	20	C	TA	SA1	28	A	TA	SA1
5	D	TB	SB2	13	D	TA	SA2	21	A	TA	SA2	29	B	TB	SB1
6	C	TB	SB2	14	A	TA	SA2	22	B	TB	SB1	30	A	TB	SB1
7	A	TA	SA2	15	B	TB	SB1	23	C	TA	SA2	31	C	TA	SA2
8	D	TA	SA2	16	C	TA	SA2	24	D	TB	SB1	32	D	TA	SA2

Topics & Subtopics

Code	Description	Code	Description
SA1	Technology & Society	SB3	Energy Power & Transportation
SA2	Pedagogical & Professional Studies	TA	Education
SB1	Information & Communication Technologies	TB	Technology
SB2	Manufacturing & Construction		

CONTINUE ▶

TEST DIRECTION

DIRECTIONS

Read the questions carefully and then choose the ONE best answer to each question.

Be sure to allocate your time carefully so you are able to complete the entire test within the testing session. You may go back and review your answers at any time.

You may use any available space in your test booklet for scratch work.

Questions in this booklet are not actual test questions but they are the samples for commonly asked questions.

This test aims to cover all topics which may appear on the actual test. However some topics may not be covered.

Studying this booklet will be preparing you for the actual test. It will not guarantee improving your test score but it will help you pass your exam on the first attempt.

Some useful tips for answering multiple choice questions;

- Start with the questions that you can easily answer.

- Underline the keywords in the question.

- Be sure to read all the choices given.

- Watch for keywords such as NOT, always, only, all, never, completely.

- Do not forget to answer every question.

1

What is the other term for a computer's main memory?

A) Secondry storage
B) Primary storage
C) Auxiliary storage
D) Reserved storage

2

Which of the following assessment methods is best in the year-long evaluation of student's drafting skills development?

A) Teacher-created assessment
B) Short-answer unit assessment
C) Baseline assessment
D) Portfolio assessment

3

Which of the following is the structure that provides vertical support in the construction of a house?

A) Headers
B) Studs
C) Joists
D) Rafters

4

In designing a doghouse, which of the following would be the first step in the design process?

A) Purchasing the required materials for building
B) Determine the measurement of the dog and the materials for the interior
C) Acquiring the necessary tools for building
D) Identifying the aesthetic concerns of the exterior

5

Which of these is acceptable according to design specifications indicating a width of 8.00 cm ± 0.05 cm and a length of 14.95 cm ± 0.10 cm?

A) 7.90 cm × 15.00 cm
B) 7.95 cm × 15.00 cm
C) 7.95 cm × 15.10 cm
D) 7.90 cm × 15.10 cm

6

Which of the following is chiefly responsible for the forward movement of a fixed-wing aircraft?

A) Thrust
B) Lift
C) Weight
D) Drag

7

Which of the following is the encoding of the signal that travels from a television remote to the television?

A) Visible light pulse
B) Series of intense infrared beams
C) Series of infrared pulses
D) Radio wave signal

8

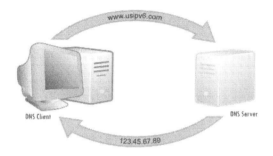

What is the role of a Domain Name System (DNS)?

A) It translates a domain name into a binary.
B) It translates a domain name into a hex.
C) It translates a domain name into an IP.
D) It translates a domain name into a URL.

9

Which of the following is most commonly used for providing the structural strength of truss bridges?

A) Rectangular units
B) Hexagonal units
C) Circular units
D) Triangular units

10

What does an effective vision statement focus on?

A) Promotion of community diversity
B) Teamwork between teachers and students
C) Continuous professional development of the school's teachers and other staff
D) High expectations for student learning

11

Engineering is defined as _____.

A) A branch of science and technology that deals with designing, building and using structures and machines.
B) A branch of science that deals with investigating the fundamental laws of the universe.
C) A branch of science that deals with the operations of machines.
D) None of the above.

12

Which of the following the potential difference of an external circuit that has a current of 2.0 A and a resistance of 7.0 Ω?

A) 9.0 V
B) 0.28 V
C) 14.0 V
D) 3.5 V

13

Which of the following is not considered as a use of standardized assessments?

A) To evaluate whether students have learned what they are expected to learn
B) To determine whether educational policies are working as intended
C) To identify gaps in student learning and academic progress
D) To use standardized test results to alter classroom curriculum

Bill wants to design a technology education program with the goal of helping students in the development of creative technical solutions to current and future societal problems.

Which of the following objectives is most appropriate for Bill's program?

A) The design and construction of a 3D model for a low-income multidwelling unit (MDU)
B) The identification of important equipment used in the construction of highways
C) The description of careers in construction related to home building
D) The categorization of components in a technical system

Gestalt psychology is a movement in psychology founded in Germany in 1912, seeking to explain perceptions in terms of gestalts rather than by analyzing their constituents and an attempt to understand the laws behind the ability to acquire and maintain meaningful perceptions in a chaotic world.

Which of the following statements would be in agreement with Gestalt theory?

A) Single notes must remain constant to recognize an overall melody.
B) Pieces of a puzzle take priority over the total image.
C) Perceptual experience is more than the sum of its elements.
D) Slower the image projection faster the perception of movement.

CONTINUE ▶

16

An operating system (OS) is system software that manages computer hardware and software resources and provides common services for computer programs.

Which of the following is NOT a function of the Operating System?

A) Memory management
B) Database management
C) Process management
D) Disk management

17

Which of the following about intelligence and creativity development of a child is not correct?

A) The Theory of Multiple Intelligences was proposed by Gardner.
B) Intelligence remains stable but IQ scores drop with age.
C) The Fagan test evaluates an infant's intelligence through her socio-motor skills.
D) IQ scores fluctuate during adolescence.

18

A hard drive is a non-volatile memory hardware device that permanently stores and retrieves data on a computer. The IBM PC-XT was the first to include a hard drive. What was the capacity of this disk?

A) 1.44 KB
B) 10 KB
C) 750 KB
D) 20 KB

19

When selecting reading materials to support the concepts presented in a lesson, a teacher should ask which of the following questions first?

A) Are these materials usable for more than one lesson presentation?
B) Will students require additional instruction to use these materials effectively?
C) Do these materials support a variety of student groupings?
D) Are these materials consistent with the students' comprehension and skill levels?

CONTINUE ▶

20

Temperature changes affect the structural properties of metals. For example, higher temperatures increase the kinetic energy of electrons whereas lower temperatures decrease electron speed.

Which of the following materials is least affected by temperature changes?

A) Germanium
B) Silicon
C) Copper
D) Carbon

21

_____ is associated in the processing of comparison speed. It has become not a measure of instruction execution speed, but task performance speed compared to a reference.

A) CPS
B) FFTS
C) MIPS
D) MPG

22

Which of the following is not a correct explanation?

A) Metacognition means thinking and learning about one's own thinking and learning processes.
B) Schema is a term used by Piaget referring to a mental construct that one forms to understand the environment.
C) Assimilation happens when the existing schema needs to be modified to take in new information.
D) Self-efficacy is a term used by Bandura for self-confidence in one's ability to complete a specific task.

23

Which situations ALL demonstrate productive use of technology as classroom tools?

A) Using interactive whiteboards in teaching interactive lessons; teaching a lesson through film-showing; encouraging the use of social media among teachers and students
B) Using interactive whiteboards in teaching interactive lessons; showing funny movies to students during their free time; showing presentations to aid teaching
C) Using interactive whiteboards in teaching interactive lessons; teaching a lesson through film-showing; showing presentations to aid teaching
D) Using technology to keep students busy; teaching a lesson through film-showing; showing presentations to aid teaching

24

The Cold War is the name given to the relationship that developed primarily between the USA and the USSR after World War Two. The Cold War was to dominate international affairs for decades and many major crises occurred, such as the Cuban Missile Crisis, Vietnam, Hungary and the Berlin Wall being just some. Which of the following options was the technology that advanced the most during this?

A) Information
B) Agricultural
C) Manufacturing
D) Military and science

25

Worm software mostly relies on security failures on the target computer to access it.

Which of the following best describes the malicious nature of worm software?

A) Sending data from a host computer to another unauthorized entity
B) Deleting or altering essential files stored on an infected computer
C) Self-replicating in order to spread across networks to other computers
D) Giving a remote hacker unauthorized access to a network computer

26

Demographic transition (DT) refers to the transition from high birth and death rates to lower birth and death rates as a country or region develops from a pre-industrial to an industrialized economic system. Which of the options from below can be considered as a supposition of the demographic transition theory?

A) Innovation and increased productivity are being promoted by population growths.
B) Levels of population and resources are proportional to rates of population growth.
C) A society's levels of technological and economic development are reflected by population patterns.
D) Food supplies increase arithmetically, and human population increases geometrically.

27

Curriculum guides are documents used by states, school districts and individual schools to guide teachers in their instruction.

Many guides are detailed, giving teachers a specific scope of what to teach and when. Many provide additional resources, such as necessary materials and assessment tools.

Which of the following about curriculum guides is not correct?

A) It helps teachers decide what to teach and when

B) It can be based on grade level of students

C) It can not be based on the number of students in each class

D) It helps teachers decide on classroom management strategies

28

A word processor is an electronic device or computer software application, that performs the task of composing, editing, formatting, and printing of documents.

Which of the following is NOT a feature of a word processor?

A) Sending email

B) Borders and shading

C) Mail Merge and letter assistant

D) Macros

29

School district supplies teachers with curriculum and necessary documents. Why should teachers still prepare annual and unit plans?

A) It is not necessary to develop annual and unit plans.

B) All school districts force teachers to write and submit annual and unit plans.

C) While preparing annual and unit plans by their own, teachers better understand what to teach.

D) Textbooks may not address all required standards, and teachers might have to supplement the curriculum.

30

Validity is defined as _____.

A) the degree to which an assessment tool produces stable and consistent results

B) the extent to which a test (such as a chemical, physical, or scholastic test) accurately measures what it is supposed to measure

C) the extent to which an assessment measures the achievement of desired objectives

D) the extent to which an assessment covers all the items that have been taught or studied.

Ms. Stanley is being interviewed for a teaching position. The school principal asked her how technology can be a useful tool for students.

Which of the ideas below should Ms. Stanley respond to give the most accurate and complete answer?

A) Technology can be used to replace the instructional role of teachers, for practicing academic skills, and for playing games.
B) Technology can be used to make learning fun, to access social media, and for practicing academic skills.
C) Technology can be used as a tool for learning new things, demonstrating knowledge and practicing academic skills.
D) Technology can be used as a tool for learning new things.

Algorithm is a process or set of rules to be followed in calculations or other problem-solving operations, especially by a computer.

A student has a horizontal list of numbered cards and sorts them manually by moving the cards in the sequence below.

1. Find the smallest card in the list and exchange it with the first card in the list.
2. Find the next smallest card in the list and exchange it with the second card in the list.
3. Repeat these instructions until the original list is sorted.

Which of the following algorithms is described above?

A) Merge sort
B) Selection sort
C) Bubble sort
D) Insertion sort

SECTION 4

#	Answer	Topic	Subtopic	#	Answer	Topic	Subtopic	#	Answer	Topic	Subtopic	#	Answer	Topic	Subtopic
1	B	TB	SB1	9	D	TB	SB2	17	C	TA	SA2	25	C	TB	SB1
2	D	TA	SA2	10	D	TA	SA1	18	B	TA	SA1	26	C	TA	SA1
3	B	TB	SB2	11	A	TB	SB1	19	D	TA	SA2	27	D	TA	SA2
4	B	TB	SB2	12	C	TB	SB3	20	C	TB	SB2	28	D	TB	SB1
5	B	TB	SB2	13	D	TA	SA2	21	C	TB	SB1	29	D	TA	SA2
6	A	TB	SB2	14	A	TA	SA2	22	C	TA	SA2	30	B	TA	SA2
7	C	TB	SB1	15	C	TA	SA2	23	C	TA	SA2	31	C	TA	SA2
8	C	TB	SB1	16	B	TB	SB1	24	D	TA	SA1	32	B	TB	SB1

Topics & Subtopics

Code	Description	Code	Description
SA1	Technology & Society	SB3	Energy Power & Transportation
SA2	Pedagogical & Professional Studies	TA	Education
SB1	Information & Communication Technologies	TB	Technology
SB2	Manufacturing & Construction		

CONTINUE ▶

TEST DIRECTION

DIRECTIONS

Read the questions carefully and then choose the ONE best answer to each question.

Be sure to allocate your time carefully so you are able to complete the entire test within the testing session. You may go back and review your answers at any time.

You may use any available space in your test booklet for scratch work.

Questions in this booklet are not actual test questions but they are the samples for commonly asked questions.

This test aims to cover all topics which may appear on the actual test. However some topics may not be covered.

Studying this booklet will be preparing you for the actual test. It will not guarantee improving your test score but it will help you pass your exam on the first attempt.

Some useful tips for answering multiple choice questions;

- Start with the questions that you can easily answer.

- Underline the keywords in the question.

- Be sure to read all the choices given.

- Watch for keywords such as NOT, always, only, all, never, completely.

- Do not forget to answer every question.

1

In a vehicle, which system provides the vehicle necessary power for movement?

A) Control
B) Propulsion
C) Guidance
D) Structural

4

Which type of wall provides the support needed to withstand weight from a building's ceiling and roof?

A) Stud-support
B) Rafter-plate
C) Load-bearing
D) Ceiling-joist

2

Which of the following file extensions should be checked when scanning for viruses in a drive?

A) .wav (Audio File Format)
B) .exe (Executable File Format)
C) .pdf (Portable Document Format)
D) .jpg (Joint Photographic Experts Format)

5

What does the acronym CRM mean?

A) Customer Relationship Management
B) Customer's Relative Meet
C) Customer Retention Manager
D) Channel Root Market Customer

3

Which of these is acceptable according to design specifications indicating a width of 8.00 cm ± 0.05 cm and a length of 14.95 cm ± 0.10 cm?

A) 7.90 cm × 15.00 cm
B) 7.95 cm × 15.00 cm
C) 7.95 cm × 15.10 cm
D) 7.90 cm × 15.10 cm

6

A protocol is a standard used to define a method of exchanging data over a computer network. Which of the protocols below is used for sending email?

A) HTTP
B) TCP/IP
C) SMTP
D) FTP

7

Which of the following explains why wind energy is viewed as a type of solar energy?

A) Solar energy is accountable for wind energy.
B) Areas rich in solar energy are also rich in wind energy.
C) Both solar and wind energies are acquired from atmospheric conditions.
D) Both solar and wind energies are renewable.

8

Which of the following is most commonly used for providing the structural strength of truss bridges?

A) Rectangular units
B) Hexagonal units
C) Circular units
D) Triangular units

9

In a large-scale commercial construction venture, which of the following is normally the first step that needs to be taken?

A) Applying for building permits and variances
B) Holding a discussion with the developer, designer, and contractor regarding the scope of the construction
C) Ordering the necessary materials for building the foundation
D) Drafting a contract specifying details of the building plan

10

Traditional manufacturing process is known for its products being made in batches. Production of the product moves from one stage to the next stage one piece at a time. One piece movement benefits the manufacturer because there is no idle time between the units. What is this process also known as?

A) One-piece flow
B) Flexible manufacturing
C) Automatic manufacturing
D) Multiple flow

CONTINUE ▶

11

Like any other equipment, computer needs special care and attention in order to perform properly and safely.

Which of the following statement is not included in a "special care" to ensure that data saved on your CD/DVD is preserved?

A) Clean the CD/DVD with a brush, in an outward direction from the centre of the disk, avoiding circular movements, to remove dust
B) Do not expose your CD/DVD to extreme temperature
C) Do not write on the reflective coating of the CD/DVD and use only recommended marker for any labelling on the label side
D) Store them in their casing – any scratch makes it difficult to read through the reflective coating

12

Temperature changes affect the structural properties of metals. For example, higher temperatures increase the kinetic energy of electrons whereas lower temperatures decrease electron speed.

Which of the following materials is least affected by temperature changes?

A) Germanium
B) Silicon
C) Copper
D) Carbon

13

Which of the following is not true?

A) The most significant quality of a good assessment is validity.
B) An assessment is the process of gathering and discussing information from multiple and diverse sources in order to develop a deep understanding of what students know, understand, and can do with their knowledge as a result of their educational experiences.
C) A standardized test is any form of test that requires all test takers to answer the same questions, or a selection of questions from common bank of questions.
D) While interpreting raw scores, knowledge of basic statistics is essential.

14

Materials-handling equipments are used across the stages of manufacturing and distributing to the disposal of products.

Which of the following guidance systems is mainly materials-handling?

A) Railroad
B) Escalator
C) Conveyor
D) Highway

15

The cache is a space in your computer's hard drive and in RAM memory where your browser saves copies of previously visited Web pages.

Which of the following statements is true?

A) L2 cache is faster than L1 cache
B) A cache hit indicates that the information we are looking for is not in the cache
C) The Internet can also be used as a cache memory
D) There are several levels of cache in a computer

16

_____ is used for connecting a local area network using one protocol with a wide area network using a different protocol. It performs the traffic directing functions on the Internet.

A) Switch
B) Hub
C) Router
D) Server

17

Wireless service is a service offering the transmission or receipt of messages by wireless telegraphy or telephony.

Current trends in the field of IT aim at providing wireless services to people while improving on the speed and storage space of existing computer systems. The term 'wireless services' means _____.

A) Without cables
B) Increase of the memory of the computer
C) Reduction in the size of computers
D) Reduction in cost of computers

18

BIOS is a set of instructions that run to help load the operating system. Which of the following is the operation of replacing the BIOS instructions stored on the ROM by a set of more efficient ones?

A) Flashing the BIOS
B) Changing the BIOS
C) Clearing the BIOS
D) Deleting the BIOS

19

Mark intends to build a garage and is determining the materials he needs for the garage's floor. It is important that the material Mark chooses should be resistant to which of the following?

A) Shear
B) Torsion
C) Tension
D) Compression

20

A third-generation programming language is a generational way to categorize high-level computer programming languages.

Which of the following is NOT a 3rd generation programming language?

A) FORTRAN
B) Java
C) ADA
D) Assembly Language

21

Which of the following is the estimated power dissipation of an electrical circuit comprising a battery with 12 volts that is connected to two 7 ohms resistors in series?

A) 168 watts
B) 1.75 watts
C) 10 watts
D) 20 watts

22

Syntax error is a character or string incorrectly placed in a command or instruction that causes a failure in execution. _____ is a process of testing a program for any syntax or logic errors.

A) editing
B) double checking
C) decoding
D) debugging

23

The hexadecimal numeral system is a numeral system made up of 16 symbols. The standard numeral system is called decimal and uses ten symbols.

The decimal value of 30 in Hexadecimal is _____.

A) 11010
B) 1E
C) 30
D) 1C

24

Fault tolerance is the property that enables a system to continue operating properly in the event of the failure of some of its components.

A plan for ensuring the fault tolerance of a computer network would most likely contain a strategy for _____.

A) Increasing the network bandwidth
B) Encrypting the most sensitive data
C) Maintaining uninterrupted power
D) Installing a proxy server on the host

25

CAD, or computer-aided design and drafting (CADD), is the use of computer technology for design and design documentation.

Which one is best suited for use with paper of large size and for complex drawings in Computer Aided Design?

A) Laser printer
B) Dot-Matrix printer
C) Ink-Jet printer
D) Pen plotter

26

In a manufacturing laboratory, a student asks his teacher what assembly procedures should be used when solving a fabrication problem.

Which of the following would be the teacher's best response?

A) Provide possible assembly procedures for the student to select
B) Ask the student to make their own judgment and decide
C) Provide an opinion on the best assembly procedure for the problem
D) Use leading questions to guide the student in analyzing the merits of different assembly procedures

27

Computer memory is any physical device capable of storing information temporarily or permanently.

Which of the following gives a list of memory in increasing order (slow to fast) of speed access?

A) L1 Cache, RAM, Hard Disk, L2 Cache
B) Hard Disk, RAM, L2 Cache, L1 Cache
C) L1 Cache, L2 Cache, RAM, Hard Disk
D) RAM, Hard Disk, L1 Cache, L2 Cache

28

Antibiotics are medicines used to treat a wide variety of infections or diseases caused by bacteria, such as respiratory tract infections, urinary tract infections, skin infections and infected wounds. Antibiotics have had both positive and negative impacts on society. Which of the following can be considered as a negative impact?

A) New types of cancers have developed due to extensive use of antibiotics.
B) Over-abundance of medical professionals.
C) Increased obesity in humans due to use in consumer products.
D) Resistant strains of bacteria caused by extensive use of antibiotics.

29

Information technology (IT) is the application of computers to store, study, retrieve, transmit, and manipulate data or information, often in the context of a business or other enterprise.

The term "Information Technology" can be summarized as:

A) Computers + Network
B) Hardware + Software
C) Computers + Connectivity
D) Connectivity + Hardware

30

Which of the following about basic terms of development is not correct?

A) Nurture refers to the effect of the environment upon a person.
B) Nature refers to the traits that are inherited.
C) Maturation is limitless but Growth is limited.
D) Learning new skills is an example of growth.

31

A high-level language is a programming language that enables a programmer to write programs that are more or less independent of a particular type of computer while machine language is a set of instructions executed directly by a computer's central processing unit.

In programming, converting high level language into machine language is done by _____.

A) converters
B) drivers
C) translators
D) service programs

32

A translator is a computer program that performs the translation of a program written in a given programming language into a functionally equivalent program in a different ways computer language, without losing the functional or logical structure of the original code.

The translator that converts high-level languages, one statement at a time into machine code, before the programme is executed is _____.

A) compiler
B) query language
C) BASIC
D) interpreter

CONTINUE ▶

SECTION 5

#	Answer	Topic	Subtopic	#	Answer	Topic	Subtopic	#	Answer	Topic	Subtopic	#	Answer	Topic	Subtopic
1	B	TB	SB3	9	B	TB	SB2	17	A	TB	SB1	25	D	TB	SB1
2	B	TB	SB1	10	A	TB	SB2	18	A	TB	SB1	26	D	TB	SB2
3	B	TB	SB2	11	A	TB	SB1	19	D	TB	SB2	27	B	TB	SB1
4	C	TB	SB2	12	C	TB	SB2	20	D	TB	SB1	28	D	TA	SA1
5	A	TA	SA1	13	D	TA	SA2	21	C	TB	SB3	29	A	TB	SB1
6	C	TB	SB1	14	B	TB	SB2	22	D	TB	SB1	30	D	TA	SA2
7	A	TB	SB3	15	D	TB	SB1	23	B	TB	SB1	31	C	TB	SB1
8	D	TB	SB2	16	C	TB	SB1	24	C	TB	SB1	32	A	TB	SB1

Topics & Subtopics

Code	Description	Code	Description
SA1	Technology & Society	SB3	Energy Power & Transportation
SA2	Pedagogical & Professional Studies	TA	Education
SB1	Information & Communication Technologies	TB	Technology
SB2	Manufacturing & Construction		

CONTINUE ▶

90334146R00036